T0086321

WHO ARE YOU?

WHO ARE YOU?

LINDA BRIDGES

WHO ARE YOU?

Copyright © 2021 Linda Bridges.

All rights reserved. No part of this book may be used or reproduced by any means, graphic, electronic, or mechanical, including photocopying, recording, taping or by any information storage retrieval system without the written permission of the author except in the case of brief quotations embodied in critical articles and reviews.

iUniverse books may be ordered through booksellers or by contacting:

iUniverse
1663 Liberty Drive
Bloomington, IN 47403
www.iuniverse.com
844-349-9409

Because of the dynamic nature of the Internet, any web addresses or links contained in this book may have changed since publication and may no longer be valid. The views expressed in this work are solely those of the author and do not necessarily reflect the views of the publisher, and the publisher hereby disclaims any responsibility for them.

Any people depicted in stock imagery provided by Getty Images are models, and such images are being used for illustrative purposes only.
Certain stock imagery © Getty Images.

All Bible verses are taken from the King James Version of the Bible.

ISBN: 978-1-6632-2303-6 (sc)
ISBN: 978-1-6632-2304-3 (e)

Library of Congress Control Number: 2021910492

Print information available on the last page.

iUniverse rev. date: 04/14/2023

ACKNOWLEDGMENT

I would like to express my thanks of gratitude to our Heavenly Father. Who through the empowerment of His Spirit encourages me to write. To be bold and share the writing. All praises and glory are given in this book to my Lord and Savior Jesus name. The Holy Spirit informed me that the name Jesus was a stranger on the little one's lips; they must know the Lord that love them more than their parents. It's for their salvation and divine protection.

In Jesus' name I pray for all who read this book to be encouraged in their hope and faith in the living Word; I pray endurance upon them, and a prepared heart for them to receive what Jesus have for them while there is time. I pray that reading this book brings much enlightenment and encouragement. I encourage you to pray for holy understanding. I rebuke and bind the spirit of fear, distraction, delay, confusion, and laziness and release the spirit of wisdom in Jesus' name. I ask the Lord Jesus to instill in you His love, power, determination, endurance, faith, and peace. Blessings to you.

I thank you, Lord, for the persons reading this book. That this book will be a blessing to them. I pray that the anointing of the Holy Ghost will be upon them to teach them, to empower, to encourage, to enlighten (for we are not ignorant of the enemy devices), in their faith in You. Now I cover the book and the people reading this book and those around them with the blood of Jesus. I rebuke and bind every Satanic interference, every demise, and traffic attack, that want to interrupt the blessing of this book I pray now in Jesus' name.

I thank Him for many mentors in my life. Pastor Ary Ross, Lula M. Thames, Idella Knight, Elmer Campbell, Darlean King, and family. Yes, so many others. Thank you for your encouragements, prayers, and listening ears. Thanks to my illustrator, Bryant Gorden. Thanks to my brethren for boldly sharing their testimonies of heaven and hell.

I searched for a way to keep my grandchildren enlightened by the Word. I began to call them and read to them bedtimes stories built on the Word. It is my intention to keep the hope alive. To keep them connected to the Lord in a way their minds would hold. I realize if I was having a challenging time keeping the Word flowing to my children then other parents or grandparents were also. The Spirit led me to share.

Scripture quotations are from the Holy Bible, King James Version. They can also be found at the end of the book in letters. Pray for me as I continue to pray for you.

I dedicate this book to my grandchildren: Destiny, Daijhua, Devon, and my children Alaide, Joe, and Danielle who have grown in divine wisdom, they are a blessing.

Agape (here and after) always in Jesus' name.

KEEP THE HOPE ALIVE

Everything God made is good. We're all beautiful creatures of God's. In Sin we were born and shaped with iniquity, through the cross we are changed. We are created in our fathers image. We must We must repent and go back to our first love and forever.

Everything God made is good. We are all beautiful creatures of God. In sin, we were born and shapen in iniquity. Through the cross we are redeemed and continue to be in our father's image. Out of his love, we were formed. We need to and therefore we will learn what First Love is truly about. We must release everything of this world to allowed Jesus to bring forth a faithful new creature. We must deny ourselves (flesh) and embrace the Living Word. Which is our new identity. We must be washed by the blood of the Lamb and then become new vessels for a new beginning. For example, new bottle for new wine, we are made to be holy supernatural vessel for a holy supernatural creator. We become babes in Christ because of our new beginning. We want to grow spiritually so that we pray to ascend to glory and be with Him forever.

Everybody is selling something in the world today. An impression, an idea, or a lie, and we see it taking root. Why not be impressed with God and his Beloved Son, Jesus. My soul wants this book to be to the glory of God. I was led by the Holy Spirit to write this book. I have read it to my grandchildren. The book brings in truth and makes children curious about Jesus. It allows them to be themselves and to see the purpose that God has for their life. They are not failures or mistakes. They are simply loved. I pray as the children grow up, they will understand their relationship with the Lord. Faith will not be a strange word to them. He, our Lord, wants them to have a personal relationship with Him.

It is imperative that we give to our children knowledge of God. He is the God of Abraham, Isaac, and Jacob. Some planned their children's future in or before they are in the womb. They know the daycares, schools, and sports they want them in. Let us make plans that they will have the option of eternality with Jesus. We want the real thing, success for our children; let it be Jesus. The Holy Spirit is the real author of this book, I am the oracle. Our Beloved Jesus is saying "Be ready"! May you and your love ones be bless and safe in Jesus' name.

WHO ARE YOU?

I am usually a happy person, but this week was a challenge for me as a young Christian. I hoped my friends could help me.

Oh man, what a day! Patrick is being mean to me; that's nothing new. This time we got into a fight. "I should have seen that one coming," Danielle said.

Helen doesn't want to play, and Carl has issues. He's so sensitive. He's upset because his guinea pig is not eating, and his dad will not take him to the vet. I asked him again, "What's wrong with your guinea pig?"

I have been through this with Carl before.

I wonder at one time how old is the guinea pig? So, we google the old age for a guinea pig with his age being six and a half years old.

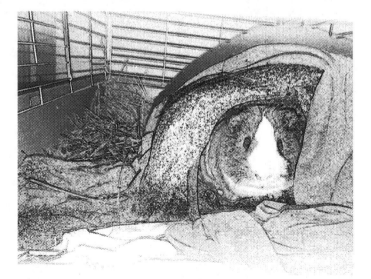

We found out that that age qualifies it as a senior citizen. When I grew up, we had a dog that died from old age, so I can relate. Mom said I bawled my eyes out. What would she expect? It was there when I was born, and I expected it to be there when I left. Anyhow the next day, I tried to play with Darlean.

Darlean likes games. I said, "Darlean, let's play." She answers, "I am PLAYING. I'm trying to finish this game. It is the best one yet." I forgot Darlean loves her electronic game more than life itself. This one was super_fast. She had to put in the missing letters before it exploded. She hated losing. I tried the game; it was too much for me.

I used to have so much fun with Mom, but not today.

My Mom is in a bad mood. What is she thinking? She let me go to the park by myself. She has not called to check up on me. I am worried. I miss Dad. He is across the sea. I don't know when he is coming home.

I am tired. I am too young for this. I'm going to lean back on this rock and rest. Because I don't know who I am.

(A) Matthew 16:15 He saith unto them, but whom say ye that I am? 16 And Simon Peter answered and said, Thou art the Christ, the Son of the living God. (Locate bible verses at the end of the book by letters)

"Who are you," said the child?

My child, you do not know me?

"No, Sir, who are you?" said the child.

God said, "My child, you do know me?"

The child said, "I met a big man before, and he scared me. I am scared of you, but I'm not afraid."

"Something is nagging me to not talk to a stranger, but I know you," said the child.

"You are big, omnipotent. I even feel you and something else. Who are you?" said the child?

"Are you Jesus? Just mentioning that Name has gotten me dirty looks because I believe in Jesus," said Danielle.

My child. Yes and no. Keep saying the Name, Jesus; keep thinking the Name, Jesus. Understanding will come.

"Whoever you are, I want to get closer. You feel good; you are smoothing. I am feeling refreshed, restored, renewed. I am tired sometimes. Can I come home to you? I barely know you, and I want to come home. Why am I telling you all of this?" said the child, Danielle.

"I know my child, but soon this too will pass. Home, you will come", said God. (B)

"Sir, I feel I should know you. It's troubling me something terrible," said the child.

"When I think that Name, the nagging voice goes away, my mind clears. Sir, who are you?" said the child. (C)

"Finally, you asked the right question from the heart. To know me is to know my Son, Jesus, and to know your origin, your root. My child, your birth, your beginning, is from Love. (D)

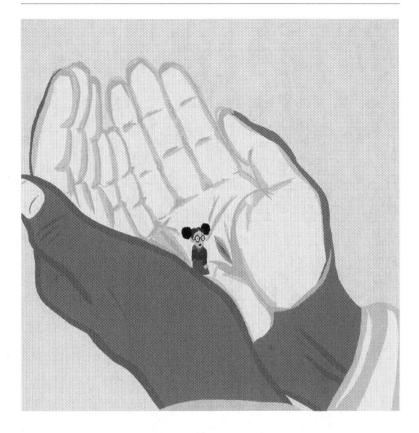

"My child, I am called by many names, but I am Love, I am your God. From me, I am your Father; I created you. I am your Creator, and from me, you are formed from Love into a soul. I am that I am; let's say there is a lot of me, and I took a tiny piece of me to form your soul. I placed you into a womb. You are a love child. You are not an accident; you are not a mistake; the Adversary planted lies (tares, weeds) among my children that are wheat. That leads to much confusion. My wheat you are. You are so dear to me." (E). "Uhm, wow!!!" said Danielle.

"I placed you in the womb," said God. "From the womb, you are born. I blew into you the breath of life. In the womb, you are molded into a vessel tabernacle not made by hand. Your flesh is mold from the clay of the earth, and in due season my child, it goes back to the earth. Remember, in my due season." (F)

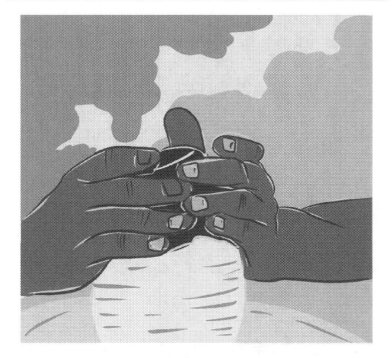

(Isaiah 64:8 But now, O Lord, you are our Father; we are the clay, and you are our potter; we are all the work of your hand.)

"The soul I created is in my image. In my image, you are created. Though you are wrapped in a fleshy clay body from the earth, the real you from your soul is the spiritual man.

You were always mine before your parents; your parents were mine before they were their parents, and so on. (G)

That is why my child, you feel you should know me. The more you think on that Name, Jesus, the moment of awareness is upon you. You know me; you are a part of me; you are loved by me, and there is so much more. Jesus is my Son. When you know Him and do know Him, you will know me. He will explain everything. He will connect you back to me. You are my child. He will do everything to get you back home to me. Trust Him, My Beloved Son, Jesus. (H, I)

"Earth was never meant to be your permanent home. Earth is not eternal; you are. There is much danger about: but in my Son is your complete protection. Stay in his Word. Stay on his Way. Stay in his Light.

Earth is your preparation place. Like a butterfly in a cocoon for a season, and it emerges beautifully with a purpose. On earth, purer than pure gold, you are to develop and transform. Whiter than snow with duty and purpose."

"There will be trials and storms, but I give guardians to all my children. If you stay in my Son's word, your guardian, an angel, will guard you and your spirit fervently. More so in these days, for some of my children are praying in my Son's name, Jesus.

They pray to me in my Son Jesus name to be bless in many ways. They pray for my angels to be loose in their life to destroy the Adversary works in Jesus' name. (J) If my Son, Jesus, is your Advocate, working for your salvation then you know there is an Adversary, the devil, causing mayhem of destruction. You cannot see it, but he is on a leash. My Son, Jesus, has all power.

My child, I want you to know that you came from heaven, and being my child, my wheat, you can go back to heaven. Your citizenship is here in heaven with me. A place prepared, not just any home but a mansion.

My child, my love, not every soul on earth is mine. They are the children of the Adversary, our enemy. But you must stay loving and wise. Wise as a serpent but gentle as a dove." (K)

"Sir, I mean, Father. Father God, I do so want to come home," said the child. I now know where this chill is coming from; why I do not fit in. Why they say it like a bad thing, you are different; I am just peculiar," said Danielle. (L)

"Yes, Sir, I remember so much. My family and I went to church some of the time. We had a hard time as a family. We love each other. Thanks to you, Father God, in Jesus' name, we did not go hungry, cold, or death did not get us early. No one, but you Lord loves us."

"Father, I see your Son's arm stretched open to me. To me, Father. I am jumping into those arms. I remember now; You bounced me on your knee. I see now, Father. I had stumbled I was holding on to the hem of Jesus' garment, slipping out of His will. I was allowing distraction and despair to lead me, and that was wrong," stated the child. (M)

"I am going to embrace Jesus, My Lord. The ride will only get rougher for now. I can see the signs in these times; I hear; I see. The Spirit speaks in a calm, still voice saying be ye ready, for I come quickly." (N)

And God said, "this is just a taste of what is in heaven. There is no bedtime for sleeping or concern about eating. Dressing, bullying, shoving, disciplining does not exist because there will be no sin in this place. There is no adulthood in heaven. Your appearance will be the best age on earth. So, there is no aging, worrying, despair, loneliness, darkness, sadness that leads to mourning or crying. No ministering will be needed. Heaven is a place of rest and peace."

"Think of the colors you can remember; there are more colors in heaven, colors we have not seen on this earth. Ever heard the wind blowing through trees, flowers, and thought you heard singing on a happy day? You might have. The flowers sing in heaven. With the Holy Spirit's eyes and ears, you will listen to wonder. In heaven, the plants sing.

Have you wondered if a family or loved ones in heaven are worrying about you on earth? There is no worry in heaven. They expect you in heaven because they know what they have planted in you—the Word of life and a pathway to heaven. You see, your "yes" will be "yes," and your "no" will be "no." There is no in_ between. Why? There is no confusion or problems in heaven. What you see is beautiful, and it is what you get. Everyone is beautiful because we are a beautiful gift from God. You have made it home." (O)

BIBLE VERSES

(Matches story by letters)

A. Matthew 16:13 When Jesus came into the coasts of Caesarea Phillippi, He asked his disciples, saying, whom do men say that I the Son of Man am? 14 And they said, some say that thou art John the Baptist: some, Elaias; and others, Jeremias, or one of the prophets. 15 He saith unto them, but whom say ye that I am? And Simon Peter answered and said, Thou art the Christ, the Son of the living God.

B. Psalm 54:4 Look, my God will help me. My Lord will support me.

Psalm 62:7 In God is my salvation and my glory: the rock of my strength, and my refuge, is in God. 8 Trust in him at all times; ye people, pour out your heart before him: God is a refuge for us. Selah.

C. John 14:6 Jesus saith unto him, I am the way, the truth, and the life: no man cometh unto the Father, but by me. 7 If ye had known me, ye should have known my Father also: and from henceforth ye know him concerning your former conduct, the old man which grows corrupt according to the deceitful lusts, 23 and be renewed in the spirit of your mind, 24 and that you put on the new man which was created according to God, in true righteousness and holiness (And put on the new nature, the regenerate self in Christ Jesus) created in God's image, (Godlike) in true righteousness and holiness.

D. Matthew 22:32 I am the God of Abraham, and the God of Isaac, and the God of Jacob? God is not the God of the dead, but of the living.

Matthew 11: 27 All things are delivered unto me of my Father: and no man knoweth the Son, but the Father; neither knoweth any man the Father: save the Son, and he to whomsoever the Son will reveal him.

E.   Exodus 34:5 And the Lord passed before him and proclaimed, "The Lord, the Lord God, merciful and gracious, longsuffering, and abounding in goodness and truth, 7 keeping mercy for thousands, forgiving iniquity and transgression and sin, by no means clearing the guilty, visiting the iniquity of the fathers upon the children and the children's children to the third and the fourth generation." 8 So Moses made haste and bowed his head toward the earth, and worshiped. (God have been describe in the Old Testament as an angel, a fire, pillar of cloud, a blinding light, a small voice, manifesting or revealing Yahweh, Jehovah, the Lord of Hosts).

F.   Psalm 139:16 Thine eyes did see my substance, yet being unperfect: and in thy book all my members were written, which in continuance were fashioned, when as yet there was none of them.

G.   Jeremiah 1:5 Before I formed thee in the belly, I knew thee; and before thou camest forth out of the womb I sanctified thee, and I ordained thee a prophet unto the nations.

H.   Ephesians 4:4 According as he hath chosen us in him before the foundation of the world, that we should be holy and without blame before him in love: 5 Having predestinated us unto the adoption of children by whom also we have obtained an inheritance, being predestinated according to the purpose of him who worketh all things after the counsel of his own will:

I. Ecclesiastes 12:7 Then shall the dust return to the earth as it was: and the spirit shall return unto God who gave it.

Thessalonians 5:23 And the very God of peace sanctify you wholly; and I pray God your whole spirit and soul and body be preserved blameless unto the coming of our Lord Jesus Christ.

Hebrew 1:14 Are not all angels ministering spirits sent to serve those who will inherit salvation?

Psalms 34:7 The angel of the Lord encamps around those who fear him, and he delivers them.

J. Revelation 13:8 And all that dwell upon the earth shall worship him (beast), whose names are not written in the book of life of the Lamb slain from the foundation of the world. 9 If any man have an ear, let him hear.

K. Peter 2:9 But ye are a chosen generation, a royal priesthood, and holy nation, a peculiar people; that ye should shew forth the praises of him who hath called you out of darkness into his marvelous light;

L. Titus 3:3 For we ourselves also were sometimes foolish, disobedient, deceived serving divers lusts and pleasures, living in malice and envy, hateful, and hating one another. 4 But after the kindness and love of God our Saviour toward man appeared, 5 Not by works of righteousness which we have done, but according to his mercy he saved us, by the washing of regeneration, and renewing of the Holy Ghost; 6 Which he shed on us abundantly through Jesus Christ our Saviour; 7 That being justified by his grace, we should be made heirs according to the hope of eternal life.

M. Matthew 24:8 All these are the beginning of sorrows.

N. Revelation 21:1 Then I saw "a new heaven and a new earth," for the first heaven and the first earth had passed away, and there was no longer any sea. 2 I saw the Holy City, the new Jerusalem, coming down out of heaven from God, prepared as a bride beautifully dressed for her husband. 3 And I heard a loud voice from the throne saying, 'LOOK! God dwelling place is now among the people, and he will dwell with them. They will be his people, and God himself will be with them and be their God. 4 He will wipe every tear from their eyes. There will be no more death or mourning or crying or pain, for the old order of things has passed away. 5 And he that sat upon the throne said, Behold, I make all things new. And he said unto me, write: for these words are true and faithful.

6 And he said unto me, It is done. I am Alpha and Omega, the beginning and the end. I will give unto him that a thirst of the fountain of the water of life freely. 7 He that overcometh shall inherit all things; and I will be his God, and he shall be my son. 8 But the fearful, and unbelieving, and the abominable, and murderers, and whoremongers, and

sorcerers, and idolaters, and all liars, shall have their part in the lake which burneth with fire and brimstone: which is the second death.

O. Matthew 19:14 But Jesus said, suffer little children, and forbid them not, to come unto me: for of such is the kingdom of heaven.

P. Philippians 3:20 For our citizenship is in heaven, from which we also eagerly wait for the Savior, the Lord Jesus Christ, 21 who will transform our lowly body that it may be conformed to His glorious body, according to the working by which He is able even to subdue all things to Himself.

Feeling the POEMS,

Cause you know Jesus

Then you know who you are.

Poems straight from the heart.

Matthew 21:16

Out of the Mouth of Babes: I am That I Am

I am that I am.
I am a God that cannot be denied.
I am a God that does not lie.
I am your God, A jealous God.
I am your God I watch the land; it is in my hand.
I am your God, the Potter molding the clay.
I am your God; besides me, there is no other.

I am your God that predestinated you.
I am the God; from me you were placed in the womb.
I am the God in my image you are created.
I am the God that knew you from creation till forever.
I am the God that will hold your right hand, (Isaiah 41:13)
so, fear not I will help thee.
I am the God that will replace your fear with love, power, and a sound mind.

I am your God, searching for vessels to trust.
Vessels prepared for every good work, sanctified.
Vessels, that is holy, for I am Holy.
Vessels of integrity, planted on the Rock of Ages,
Vessels of righteousness because it embraces my Living Word.
Vessels tried by fire that abstains from wickedness.

I am that I am; I am a God of Love.
I am that God that is your Father.
I am that God, you know me.

I am that God; you deny your true self and
Do not understand me.
I am that God, a God of Wrath. I am that God that will reduce the world
to childhood.
I am that God that chastises those I love.
I am that God that will restore faith, hope, and love in my children.

I will be their light in the darkness.
I will be their way when lost.
I will be their truth that defuses the lies.
I will be their healer from the illnesses and plagues.
I will be their friend, even in the midnight hour.
I will be their bread when they are hungry.
I will be their water when they are thirsty.
In ignorance, I will show mercy.
In their foolishness, I will make them wise.
In being at the end, I will make them first.
In their death, I will give them a crown of life.
For my children, I will make known every secret.
For my children, I will unveil every mystery.
For my children, only for my children,
I will give them a love that completes them.   *Pastor Linda Bridges*

In my time of need, for such a time of this, He was and will always be with me.

Who am I say me? I am the house!

I am the tabernacle not made by hand.
I am the church.
I am a true citizen to be in heaven.
I am the bride of Christ.
I am the kingdom of God.
I am the righteousness of God in Christ.
I am a holy priest.
I am a light in this world.
I am a vessel that desires to be fitted for the Master's use.
I am born of God and the evil one does not touch me.
I am one with the mind of Christ.
I am the peace of God that surpasses all understanding.
I am a light that cannot be hidden under a bushel.
I am a vessel that greater is He Who is in me than he in this world.
I am giving, and it is given to me; good measure, pressed down, shaken together, and running over, men give into my bosom.
I am one that has not lack for God supplies all my need per His riches and glory by Christ Jesus.
I am one that can do all things through Christ Jesus who strengthens me.

I am a vessel of God who shows forth the praises of God, who hath called me out of the darkness and into His Marvelous Light.
I am joint_heir with Christ.
I am the temples of the Holy Spirit; I am not my own.

I am as small as a grain of sand on a beach.

I am as big as a star of the heaven that shines in the sky.

I am healed mentally, physically, spiritually, and thus completed by the stripes of Jesus Christ.

The blood of the Lamb redeems me.

I am not conformed to this world but transformed by the renewal of my mind by the living word.

What is the Bible?

Some say a Holy Book
Older than time itself,
It has been said to be a roadway
To show a path to heaven's doors.
To others it's a treasure map,
Street paved of gold.
To a dying man it can be said
To be a place of life abundantly.
A woman in turmoil, holding on,
A place of peace, many have known.
To a parent in despair with nowhere to go
The way to a place where tears will never flow,
And everyone eventually will want to go.
Many desires and make a start
But depart before they make the mark,
To some a calm still voice
That has all the answers.
Though it's composed of many words
It is the word.
To a parent who has lost

Their child to the street
Hope for the lost sheep.
An ark of safety to a dying world.
So, from the heart these terms have embark,
A living word from a book of life,
Strength and guidance.

A religious manual telling right from wrong
But only as good as the faith you hold on.
Words of God to perform and live by,
Life road map.
My everything putting it boldly
Infallible word of God.
Recording for daily living,
Unchanging, unrelenting, everlasting word from God.
A book of prophecy.
A book of ancient stories happening today.
Teaches about love, kindness, and life
Full of gifts from God.
Long_suffering from a sinless man
Showing the return of the prodigal son.
Life dictionary to eternal life,

How to have a relationship with God?
A mystery to those that do not know God.
Joy in time of sorrow,
Deliverance and healing with complete peace of mind.
The way teaching, inspire word of God.
Open the door to a sanctuary of peace,
Lots of love letters.
My sword and my armor
With instructions on how to use the above.
The ten commandments, that will get you home.
My insurance policy to life,
My daily bread,

My companion,
Holy Word,
The law,
My manual,
My survival kit,
Sense of fulfillment for the inner man.
My guide, my inspiration
Letters from Jesus Christ.
How to be selfless and how to treat other,

Guidance for men to do the right things;
Guidance for women to be virtuous.
Now you have heard about the word
Hide it in your heart and please only God.

Pastor Linda Bridges

I Fall on Bended Knees

Every knee shall bow.
Every tongue shall confess.
Jesus is Lord; He is Lord of my life,
For this reason, I fall on bended knees.
Everything that hath breath praise ye the Lord
Submit to His will then truly live,
Lift holy hands and praise ye the Lord
For this reason, I fall on bended knees.
When I am stressed, I give the Lord my best,
It is then, I confessed
Lord, I'm having a problem passing this test.
For this reason, I fall on bended knees.
I come before Him with a contrite heart.
I humble my being to my Lord.
My life is His; He has given me abundantly,
For this reason, I fall on bended knees.
He the Potter, I am but clay;
XXXXXXXXXXXXXXX

The bully made the earth his playground. He still was not happy. Then no one would be happy though he smiles all the time.

Norwood did not understand the bullying motive. He seemed to have everything but always wanted more. He noticed many tried to stand up to him. They were able and well_known children of integrity. They were reliable, healthy, and knew what they wanted out of their lives, but eventually, they got worn down. Some went into such despair that the fight left them. They walked the playground like zombies, an example to the rest on the playground around the bully. And this included the adults, they overlooked the bully, and he always got a free pass. It worked on me, Norwood, and I stayed conformed for a while.

Norwood watched all this daily. It occurred over and over. Norwood's mind was at an impasse on how to approach this situation. He was tired.

The girls did not fare well on the playground. They came to the playground looking one way and went to the bathroom to conform. They came in long skirts and immediately shortened it, a plain face to a made_up face; they could be humiliated, intimidated, slap on the butt, hair pull, etc. They conformed and stayed away from the bully and his group. They knew it was best to blend in and go along with the program. They did not want to be the day entertainment. It could get ugly.

There were days when no matter how hard you tried to blend in, you could get picked out to be picked on. We tried to get to the newcomers quickly and queued them on the program of the playground. It was weird how the bully always knew who the murmurs were. Many times, he quells confrontation before they happen. Everyone had to come to attention if one or more was to be bullied.

They all had to come to participate, and it felt dirty. It was dirty. Norwood knew it was only a matter of time before it was his turn. Norwood decided to do what his parents did. He thought it was old fashion, but it seems to heal his mom and dad. It kept peace in the house. So, Norwood did it. He prayed.

Norwood noticed a small group hanging around a quiet young man. More importantly, he noticed the bully never went near Him or those around Him. As a matter of fact, they broke all the bully's rules, and he did nothing. He remembered seeing them when he entered the playground, but they seemed like boring nerds, and he wanted to be in the in crowds. He saw where that got him. He did not understand why he did not notice this sooner.

By now, Norwood is tired. He wanted to change! He was desperate! He was ready to try anything to get out of the monopoly. At the end of the day, he decided to sit with the plain children tomorrow.

The next day Norwood sits with the peculiar children. He found out they were anything but boring. They were fun! The bully notice, but to Norwood surprise, did not approach him.

The Bully mission is to destroy. The quiet Guy told me the mission. It is to kill, steal, and destroy. He destroys in many ways but with us it is our self_esteem and confidence he destroys. We began to lose our innocence that is priceless. We don't know who we are anymore; we wait for someone to tell us what to do next. It starts out of fear then grows into a habit. That explained why everything good about our life was gone. We have the appearance of joy and fun, but trust me, there was neither. "I seem it for myself," said Norwood.

I stayed with the quiet Guy. He never changes and meets all my needs. It is like I have a new family. I knew it was a matter of time before the bully caught me alone. Truth be said, "I was scared, but I have Truth on my side." Later I saw him on the ground bullying the children. I knew he was not the big bad wolf he appears to be.

Yes, he caught up with me. Yes, in the bathroom. I started mumbling the truth I knew and taking a standard up against him. Though I felt frightened, I was not going to have a change of heart.

He pulls off his belt with the buckle loose. I knew what was coming, I had seen it before. His aim was to humiliate, imitate, and dominate me. In the past and in my ignorance, I allowed him to do this. This stops now! He approaches me; then he slows down.

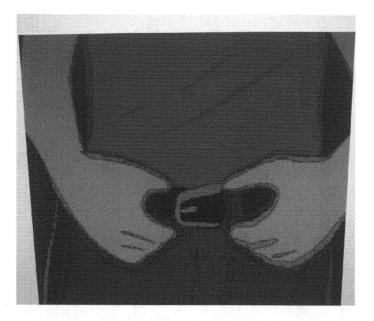

I murmur the Name. He looked at me strangely and said, not you too. He began to put the belt back on. Kept approaching me. Like we are old friends. I said the Name louder. He reminds me of the good times. I know that I never had any. He keeps approaching I open my mouth to say the Name, Jesus, loud. He grabs his chest like he was wounded. He turns around. As he was turning around, another boy was rushing in. Running into the bully and almost ran back out. But he really had to use the bathroom.

The boy lost his urge to use the bathroom. He was curious because I was still standing, no bruises, and looking strong. I was amazed at myself. I had a lot to tell him and the others. We have been going about this the wrong way. The man, name Jesus, is the way.

We stop having trouble out of the bully. We later heard he transferred. That means he is still out there somewhere. Jesus said in his word that the Bully is in check, because he is sentence and judged. It is the choices we make that put us in his control. Jesus said, "He is the Way."

John 10:27, 28

27 My sheep hear My voice, and I know them, and they follow, Me. 28 And I give them eternal life, and they shall never perish; neither shall anyone snatch them out of My hand.

John 10:10

10 The thief does not come except to steal, and to kill, and to destroy. I have come that they may have life, and that they may have it more abundantly.

John10: 29,30

29 My Father, who has given them to Me, is greater than all; and not one is able to snatch them out of My Father's hand. 30 I and My Father are one."

I DO KNOW GOD!!!

"Mom, where are we going now," said Devon.

"There is a sale," said Mom. "They're always on sale. What sale? Everything in the store is for sale," said Devon.

"Smarty pants,' said Mom. "Mom, can we go to the park," said Devon. "Not now. I have another stop to make," said Mom.

"Momma, they said do not buy up the store; leave some for other people," said Devon. "Boy, watch your mouth," Mom said. "How many stops," Devon said, "Can this be the park?"

Mom gave me a silent treatment look. Eyebrows are about to touch, and her nose is squinching in concentration. Looks like she is about to go my way.

I said, "Can the last stop be the park." And added, "it could be one of your stops," said Devon. She relaxed her face and smiled. Mom said, "I am smarty pants."

I knew Mom liked talking about God. So, I decided to try it. "I know God," Devon told Mom.

She stops at the stop sign and looks at me. She looked at me. Mom asks, "what do you know." I said, "God has a Son name, Jesus." I knew that because I pray to Him every night.

Mom took the next turn and went to the park. I was happy, but playtime was short; Mom began to ask me, "what do I know about God?" I did not suspect quiz time!

I told Mom that they told us in the church that God sent Jesus to save us because we were lost. I don't understand all of that because I know my home address and your cell number. I noticed that Jesus was the person people loved to love and then became the person people loved to hate. Then they killed Him. Somehow, He did not stay dead, so we won't either.

Mom said, "what else do you know?" I said, "He did magic; no, I mean miracles. One of the others is there a difference. Uhm, He lived like a poor man. I wonder why because his Father is from heaven? Oh yes, his father was a carpenter. Hmm mm. He healed a lot of people; people did not understand Him. He feds a lot of people to be a poor man."

"People like what Jesus did then they did not like Him. Many turned against Him. They did like the kids at school. They gamed up on Him and bullied Him. Then it gets confusing. He had all that power and did not fight back. Why Mom?" I asked.

I don't know why they have not made a video game of Jesus. They said He has all power. I try to get that power when I play my games, but I don't do well. If I play Jesus' game, I could. I could learn how to get some of that power. Mom said, "did you change the subject to a video game."

Mom said, "it's not always about getting the most power and winning. Sometimes you have to let go of all to win." "Ohm," I said.

They got so angry at Jesus that they killed him. Let me see. I'm trying to remember. I don't like this part. But they beat Him up, stabbed him, and did other things for no reason, and He died on a cross they nail Him on. The church calls it something. "It's called the Crucifixion," said Mom.

Devon asked, "Mom, why did they beat Him up?" Mom said, "It has to do with us being lost. You remember a lot. You do know God's only Son. For God so loved the world he gave his only Son. They did not understand his purpose. They were lost in the world's confusion and deception while the enemy turned people's hearts against God's Son. The enemy knew our Lord would make all things new; this would completely take away the enemy's power. And everyone would see that Jesus does have all the power."

"Lord Jesus did many good things; He did not do it their way. Jesus did not bow to their ways, nor did he not and would not sin. He was not like them or like us," said Mom.

"He came to get us back on the righteous way and home with Him. You see, we were lost. We lost our way back to heaven. Many stops believing and seeking Jesus, so they are lost. They have no faith: they stop believing because they do not know Him. Jesus stirs up the longing for home, that heaven. He made away to make us new creatures. Because of that, we can go back to our true home, heaven with Jesus and Our Father. Jesus gave us some help and that his Spirit.," said Mom.

"We desire to spend eternity with Jesus and not in this world. This life will not be forever on this earth. This earth will pass away one day. We are spiritual beings that do not pass away; when we stop breathing; we sleep. This earth will be here long enough for us to finish our journey, and our Lord will bring a new heaven and earth," said mom.

"You are an impressive young man," said Mom. "Go play on your rides. I am watching from here." "Wow!" I thought, "she would not let me ride." Out loud, I said, "thank Mom." And I ran off.

We made it home. Dad is working late. I guess Mom has to read to me. So, I said to her, "Mom are you going to read to me?" Dad let me pick out the book, but I want Mom to read it, so I tell her, "Mom, you can pick a book." She looked like she was going to say no, but she picked out a small book she liked and began to read.

I am so tired. Bath, prayed, and bed, and I did not get TV time. Well, maybe tomorrow. Mom spoke to me and said, "are you listening." I smiled and said, "Yes." She kisses me on the head, and I realize I must have fallen asleep because she has finished the book. I told her to wait, so I gave her a big hug. Now she can go to bed.

I nodded to sleep when I heard a voice say, "so you know me!" Looking to see where the voice was coming from, I wanted to thank it was daddy, but I knew it was not daddy. I am now wide awake.

"Son, you said you know me." said the Voice. I remembered my manner and said, "Yes, sir."

"Sir," I said, "Who are you?"

The Voice said, "Son, you said you knew me; that's what you told your mom. You said you prayed to me every night." My eyes were open, but they opened wider. I said, "You are Jesus, the Messiah, the Son of God!" "Yes, I am the Christ," said Jesus. "Your Mom was busy, but I noticed you cut the talk short. What do you want to talk to me about?"

Devon became speechless, which is rare for him. He noticed he was not feeling sleepy. Going back to sleep was not an option.

Devon finally said, "I kept asking in my prayers for Mom and Dad to be at home more. I stopped asking because I thought you got tired of hearing the same thing. Mom called me smarty pants, and Dad called me Bubba. I have to go out of my way to get them to pay attention to me. I'm scared; Charles' parents got a divorce. Alice's parents fight. I want mine to be happy with me."

Jesus said, "I know your heart means well. Your parents love you, and they love each other. Your bad grades are to get your parents' attention, but you are hurting yourself. Bubba, I am the God of a living word and do not lie. In love, I nurtured them and corrected my children. Young and old, I am with them as they go through their life and troubles. But there is an enemy out there that will try to destroy homes. He put things in their lives to overwhelm the family. But because they believe and seek me, they are overcomers. They survive. You continue to pray for them, knowing that I will show them the way to stay a family. It's in my love and my word. I am the way. That doesn't mean there will be no more hard times. Well, as your mom says, "trouble doesn't last always."

Devon, I enjoy our talks. I love you so much, I will never leave you or forsake you. A place here with us has already been prepared for you. As I fulfilled my purpose on earth so must you.

I send the Holy Spirit to comfort you; and guide you into truth and righteousness. You will always believe in me and that will help you keep faith in Me. Those are the only type of people that will live with me in heaven. Those that live in truth and righteous. Beware of bad company that can corrupt your mind. You do not want to lose your way home to Me.

Pray for your classmates. Your prayers go a long way, Devon. They will help many people. My children are peculiar, unique, and beautiful. They are the apple of my eye. Remember you are special to me.

Devon slept well that night. The next day Devon saw one of his friends, Jakari, in the hallway crying between classes. Devon walks him to the bathroom as Jakari explains what happened when they bullied him. They talk about his bushy eyebrows and thick curly hair. Devon told his friend to look at the facts. His friend gave a wet snotty sniff and looked at Devon. Devon said, "Jakari, we are both chubby but cute. My mom tells me all the time. I am going to grow up and lose this adorable baby fat of chubbiness. That what grown up called it." Devon takes a deep breath and sigh saying, "we are going to be some handsome dues." "We will lose our baby fat and they will gain there. You will have a head full of hair and we see who will laugh then," laugh Devon with Jakari.

Devon could tell Jakari felt better. Devon lightly said, "he had to go back to the classroom." Jakari said, "me too." Devon feeling happy could have sworn he heard a light voice saying, "my son, my son you have much to learn."

John **14** "Let not your heart be troubled; you believe in God, believe also in Me. (NKJV)

John **14** "Do not let your hearts be troubled. You believe in God; believe also in me. (NIV)

Printed in the United States
by Baker & Taylor Publisher Services